This Book belongs to:

Sadie

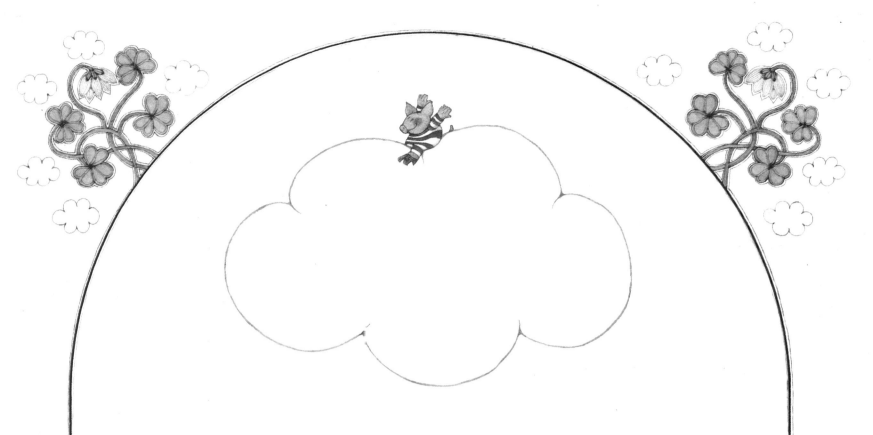

For: Sadie

Kolja, Claus, Antje, Peter, Inger, Heiner, Rosemarie, Michael, Sabine, Elisabeth, Max, Helmut, Wolfgang, Siggi, Gertrud, Sebastian, Ulle, Gudula, Stefanie, Axel, Toni, Hugo, Erika, Lutz, Monika, Boris, David, Ulla, Andrea, Uta, Krystof, Hilde, Katrinchen, Lotte, Huck, Julika, Benjamin, Katinka, Daniela, Katrin, Marco, Robert, Heike, Helga, Carl-Wilhelm, Blacky, Martin, Lucie, Vera, Carl, Eva, Patrick, Claus, Brigitte, Markus, Nicolai, Marc, Tanja, Kay, Irmtraut, Anita, Herlinde, Dietmar, Vivi, Barbara, Dieter, Jurgen, Christl, Christian, Edith, Philipp, Matthias, Florian, Jan, Klas, Heidi, Hermann, Emil, Mascha, Collin, Cay, Britta, Frederik, Anna, Dagmar, Walter, Uschi, Reimer, Kirsten, Tim, John, Ilse, Nils, Nienke, Hielian, Frank, Pieter, Schnasi, Iris, Gisela, Isabell, Inga, Fritz, Barbel, Julia, Josefine, Cornelius, Rolf, Gabi, Heinz, Geka, Ingrid, Karin, Thomas, Beate, Diana, Ralf, George, Bruni, Jochen, Ali, Uwe, Laura, Josi, Micky, Lilly, Bertel, Edgar, Horst, Icki, Jana, Astrid, Annette, Adelie, Charly, Claudine, Renate, Arno, Ulrike, Susanne, Tassilo, Manfred, Jessica, Dorothee, Hans, Bernd, Gro, Hansi, Linn, Helma, Puppa, Volker, Claes, Meike, Inka, Ellen, Felix, Doris, Patricia, Pia, Franz, Carla, Brigitta, Sven, Nina, Lisa, Swantje, Cora, Alexander, Henry, Heino, Elke, Gerold, Andreas, Angela, Angelika, Beatrix, Pit, Rosi, Jeannette, Christiane, Christine, Tina, Melanie, Claudia, Bruno, Illiana, Jupp, Madeleine, Mo, Kaspar, Moritz, Paul-Clemens, Schitti, Daniel, Natalie, Diemut, Marc-Daniel, Valerie, Frederic, Esther, Denise, Sarah, Kirsten, Alexa, Leo, Tessa, Franziska, Gudrun, Judith, Julian, Ortrud, Cornelia, Martina, Thekla, Silvia, Majja, Verena, Ossy, Nika, Annika, Maren, Bastian, Natascha, Judy, Till, Michaela, Marion, Kajo, Ingeborg, Petra, Birgit, Karola, Christa, Imme, Ina, Irene, Karoline, Marina, Sonja, Gabriele, Christoph, Itta, Karsten, Karl-Georg, Anne, Anja, Christa, Dick, Werner, Lis, Katja, Graziela, Pia, Larissa, Melanie, Tilman, Karsten, Christa, Rupert, Michelle, Juli, Claire, Colette, Ines, Christine, Claudia, Heike, Anita, Helga, Johanna, Dimitri, Gudrun, Andreina, Mira, Nicole, Ulf, Marco, Regina, Sascha, Ulrike, Ari-Daniel, Klaus-Dieter, Judith, Tilla and:

....

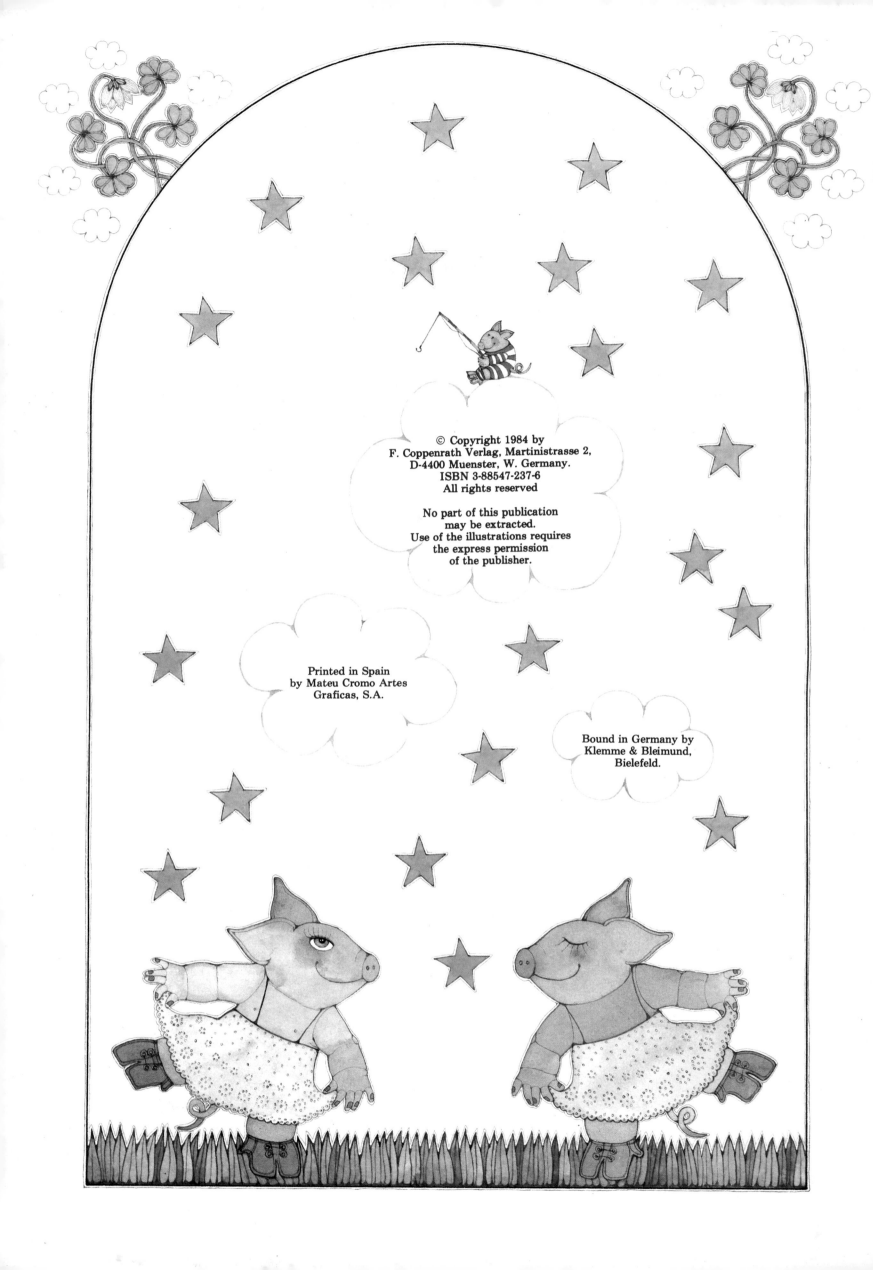

Printed in Spain
by Mateu Cromo Artes
Graficas, S.A.

Bound in Germany by
Klemme & Bleimund,
Bielefeld.

Antje Vogel

THE BIG BOOK FOR LITTLE DANCERS

The exercises were chosen and compiled by Heidi Sievert, Muenster, Germany.

Coppenrath Verlag Muenster

Dear Sadie,

In this book you will find all the exercises for an hour's ballet lesson. There are exercises for loosening up, exercises at the barre and exercises in the center — in other words, without holding on.

So — you are ready to begin . . .

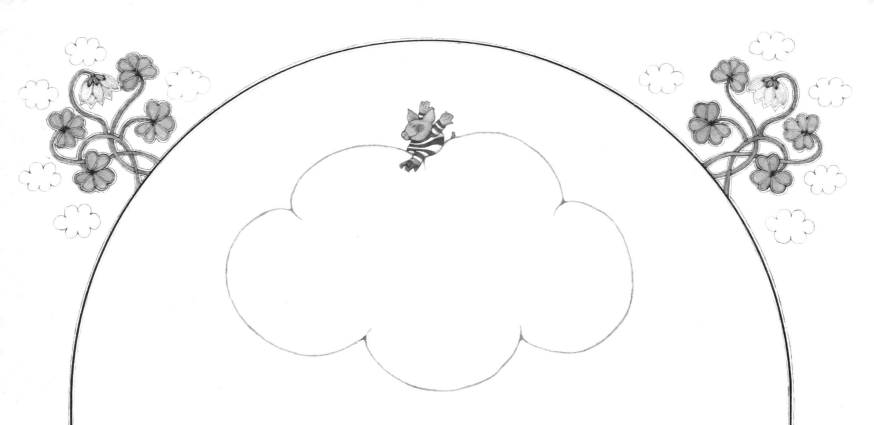

Even if you don't go to a ballet school it will be fun to practise the loosening up exercises. My son Kolja can do them and he's only five. He watched me while I was doing the drawings and immediately tried them all.

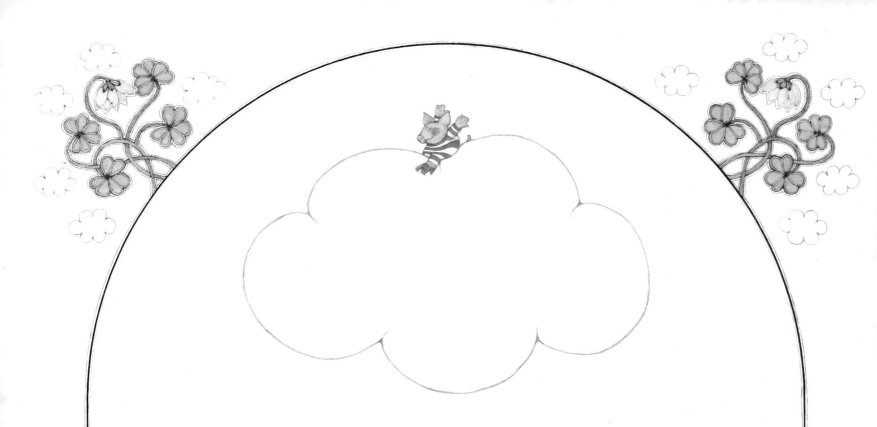

Ballet is fun! Not only that, an hour's exercises will use every muscle in the body. That makes ballet an ideal sport for children and adults alike.

Have fun!

Yours,

Antje Vogel

What do I need and when?

The tutu, a stage costume, may be needed for a performance.

A dancer needs new toe shoes for every performance because afterwards they will be worn out! But they can be mended and used for training.

Leotard

Make your own!

Legwarmers
2 knitting needles Nr.8.

Bits of old wool

Cast on about 40 stitches. Knit 2 and purl 2 until work measures about 12 inches. Cast off and sew the side seams together.

Toe shoes have a reinforced toe cap and a hard sole. You should not start to toe-dance before the age of 10-12. Before that age foot joints would be under too much strain.

Tights

Legwarmers

You start ballet school around the age of 6 and jazz ballet from about the age of 15.

Softs

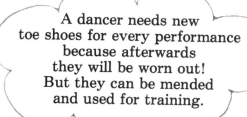

Loosening up exercises

1

Sit on the floor, feet together, knees apart. Bounce knees gently up and down while counting up to 8.

Then let your knees rest and loosely bounce your head toward your feet while counting to 8.

Now stretch your arms way up over your head. Make your back long and straight. Stretch your sides from the waist and count to 8. Gently drop your head to your feet, keeping your back round and count to 8.

Repeat both exercises alternately (one after the other).

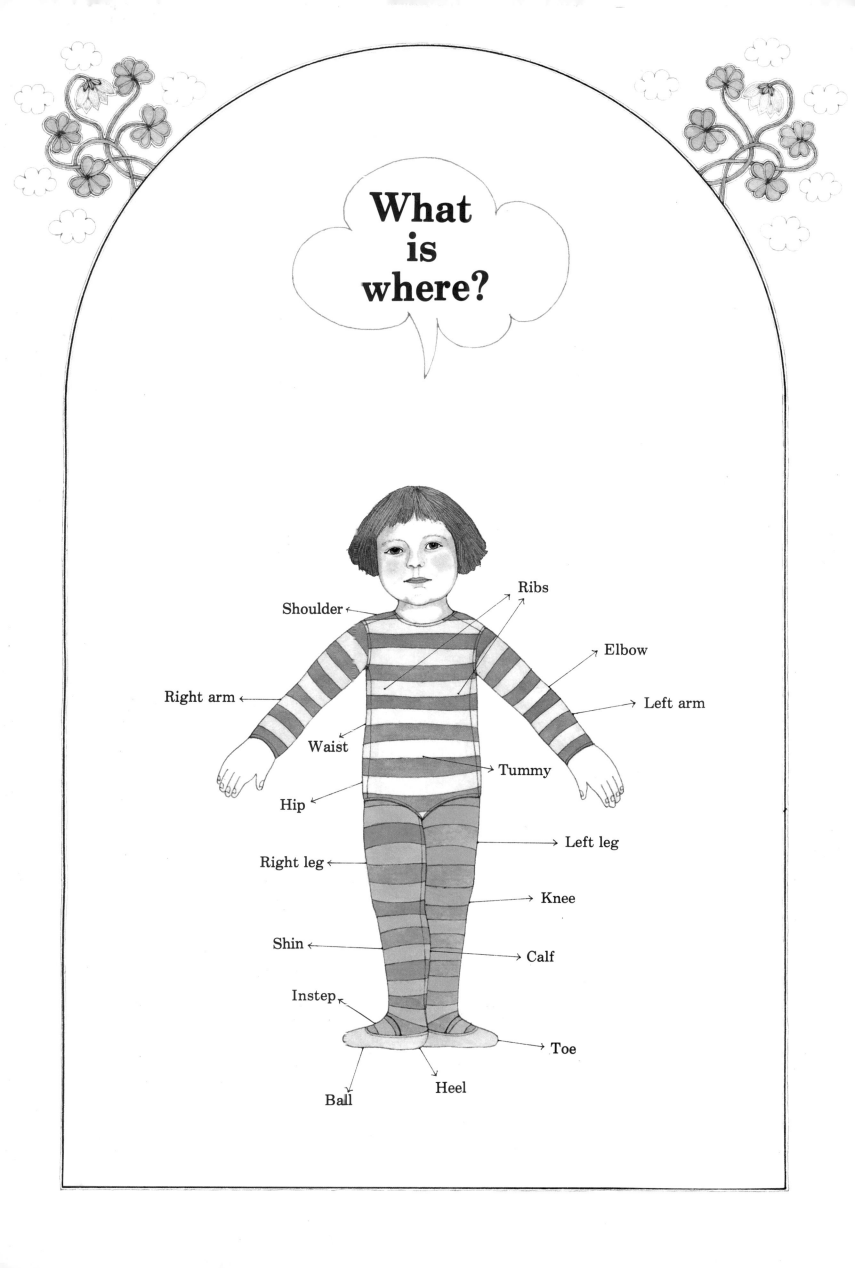

What is where?

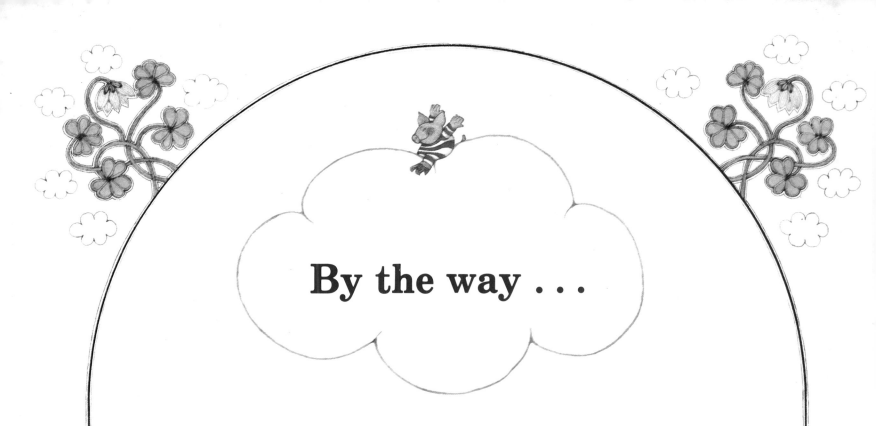

By the way . . .

The story goes that in about 1824 the ballet master Filippo Taglioni invented toe-dancing for his daughter Maria in the hope of distracting attention from her long nose!

And Maria Taglioni really did become a very famous dancer.

6

Crouch down with
your hands on the floor
in front of your feet.
Feet together.

Bounce 4 times while crouching.
Then straighten legs, keeping hands
on the floor as long as you can.
Repeat the whole exercise 4 or 8 times.
After the last time straighten up very slowly
— unroll one vertebra at a time
till your whole body is straight.

Keep
legs nice and
straight.

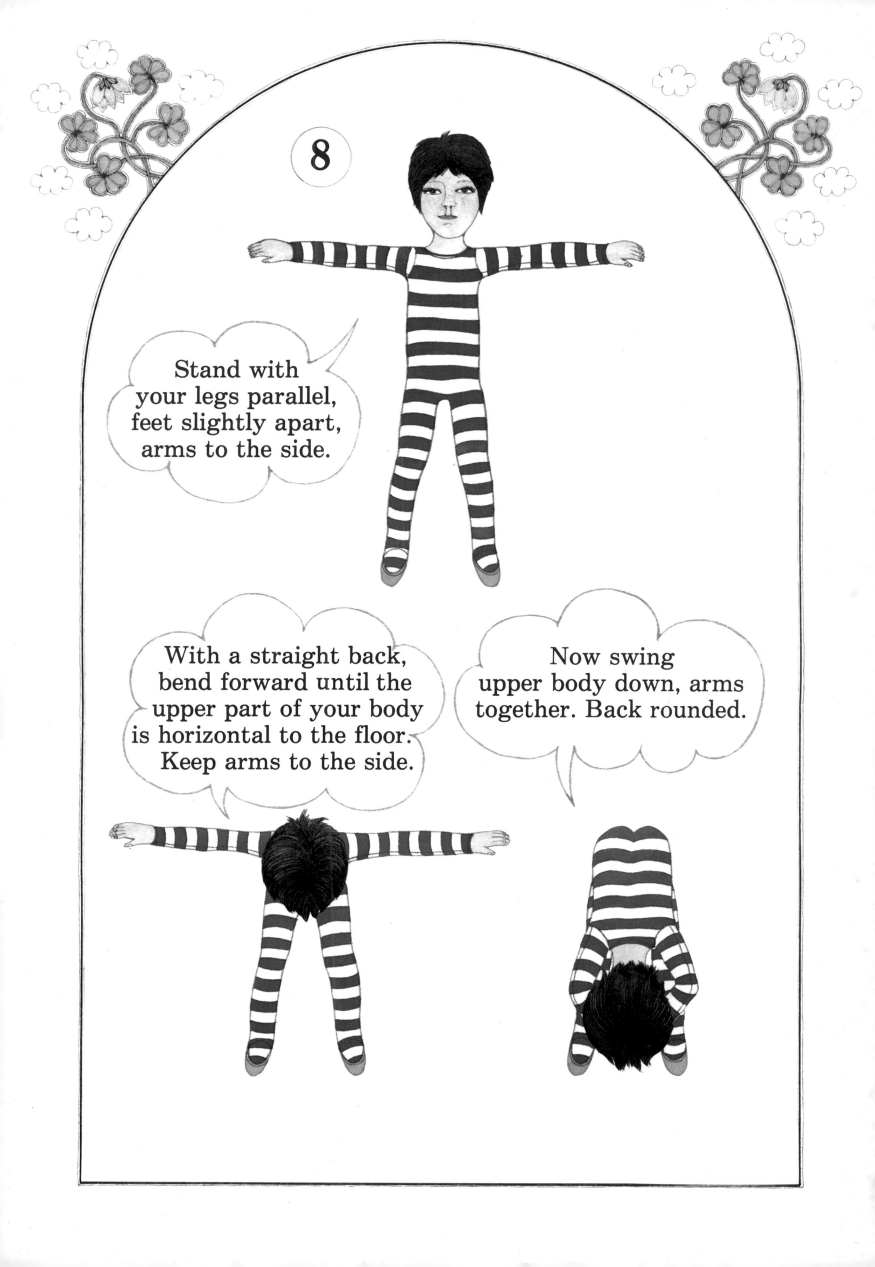

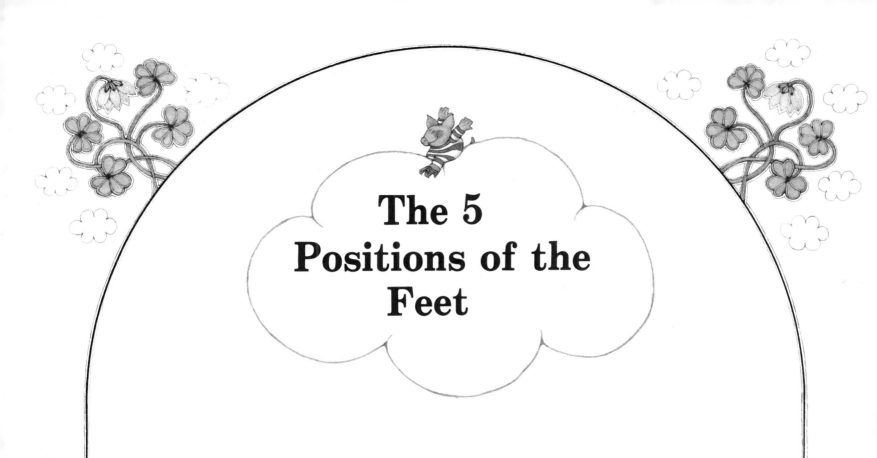

The 5 Positions of the Feet

1. With heels together turn your feet out as far as your thighs will turn. When bending your knees, they should be over your toes. All your toes should lie flat on the floor. The outer edge of the foot should carry more weight and the instep should be raised.

Very important as otherwise the knees would be damaged and it doesn't look so nice.

2. Turn thighs outward again with feet 1-1½ foot-lengths apart.

3. Put one foot halfway in front of the other with the heel of the front foot pressed against the arch of the back foot.

Beginners should only practise these three positions.

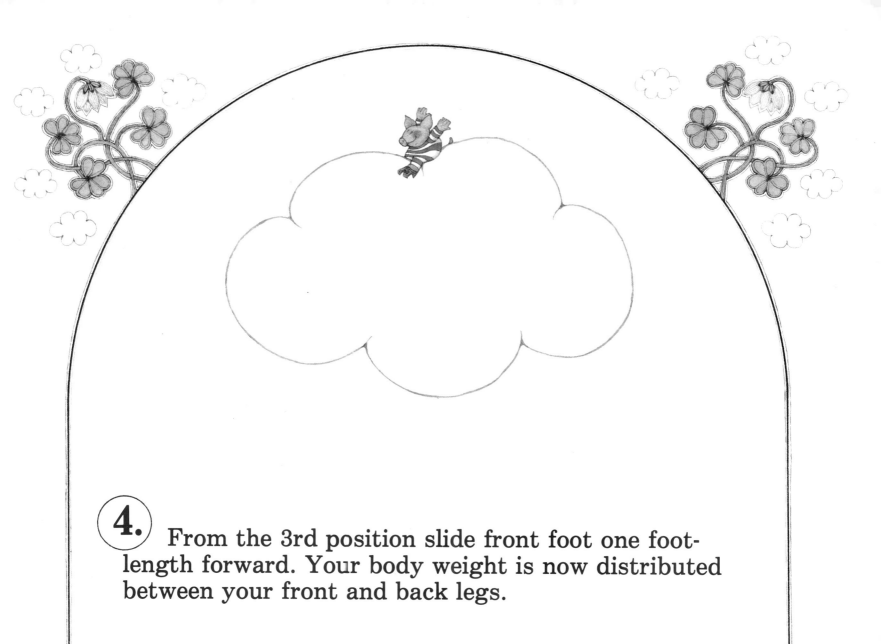

4. From the 3rd position slide front foot one foot-length forward. Your body weight is now distributed between your front and back legs.

5. Like the 3rd position except that the feet are more crossed. For the 5th position you must be well turned out from the hips, otherwise you stand flat-footed and put too much strain on your knees — and that's not healthy.

1 2 3 4 5

By the way . . .

This is the right way
to stand at the barre: one hand
is placed loosely on the barre —
right in front of your body.
Arm is almost completely straight.
Push your bottom down and draw
your tummy in – that straightens
your spine. Now stretch your
neck upwards and
lift your head.

Bend
your knees further
down into a grand-plié
lifting your heels off the
floor as far as necessary.
Come up again into a demi-
plié, quickly drop your
heels on to the floor
and straighten your
legs.

Don't go
so low to the ground that
you're sitting on your
heels.

Pliés are done one
after another in all 5 positions. In a demi-plié
the heels should always stay flat on the floor.
In a grand-plié they should stay flat only in the 2nd
position. Knees are straight over the toes. Don't go
so low that your bottom touches the ground.

3

Battement tendu jeté

Slide the right leg forward as in a battement tendu but then raise the point of your foot about 8 inches off the floor, no higher. Don't swing your leg loosely but move powerfully right to the tips of your toes — just as if you were striking a match.

To the front, to the side, to the back, to the side. Always slide back into the 1st position. Repeat on the left side

5 Rond de jambe à terre

Doing a rond de jambe
is like drawing a half circle on the
floor with a straight leg whereby the
foot is pulled along the outer edge of the
circle through into the 1st position. From
the front to the side, to the back = 'en dehors'
From the back to the side to the front
= 'en dedans'. First with the right leg,
then turn round, right hand on the
barre and work with your left leg.

1st position.

Slide the right leg forward.

Bring it to the side.

Draw a half circle to the back.

Again to the side and forward.

By the way . . .

This is what a dancer looked like 150 years ago.

Maria Taglioni. April 23rd 1804 — April 24th 1884

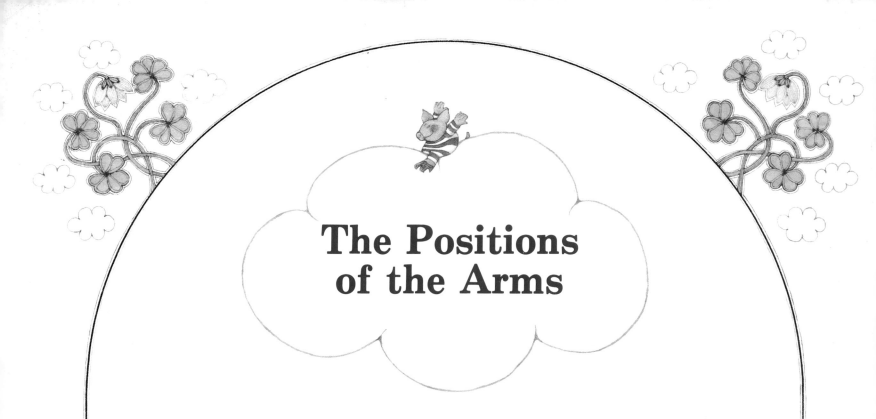

The Positions
of the Arms

Both arms down and gently curved, with fingers almost touching. Elbows slightly raised. This is the basic position or 'préparation'.

All the exercises have French names because French is the 'ballet language'.

For 1st position
raise both arms in the basic position
to chest height. Open arms to the side into
2nd position, but not too far back. Always keep the arms in front of your body otherwise you may have an arched back. You must feel the tension from one hand through the back to the other hand — without interruption! Don't draw your shoulder blades together and don't let your shoulders fall forward. Now, raise your elbows towards the back, turn hands towards the front, keeping fingers together and bring both arms above your head into 3rd position.

Préparation

Now the fingers almost touch again, arms are not directly over the head but slightly to the front, shoulders stay low.

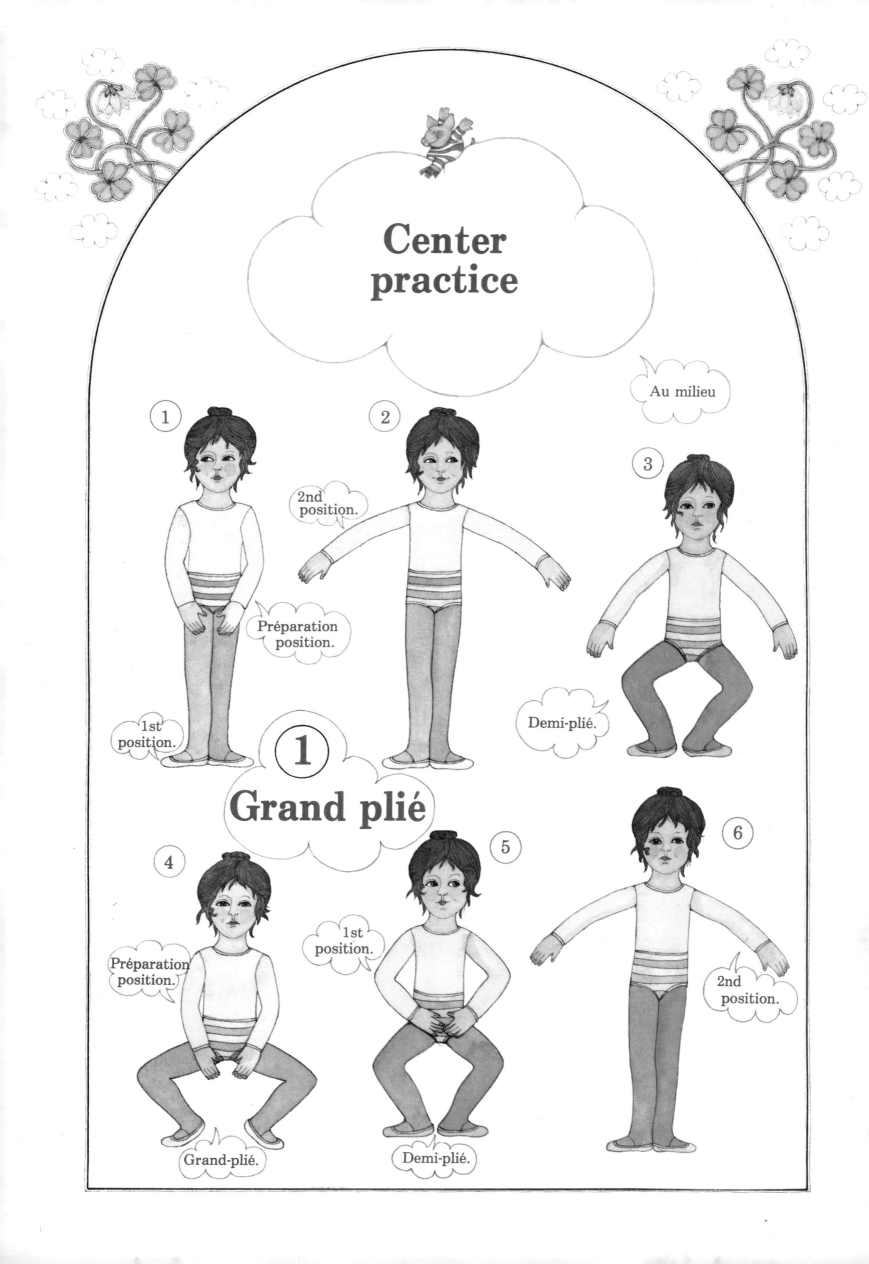

5
Arabesque

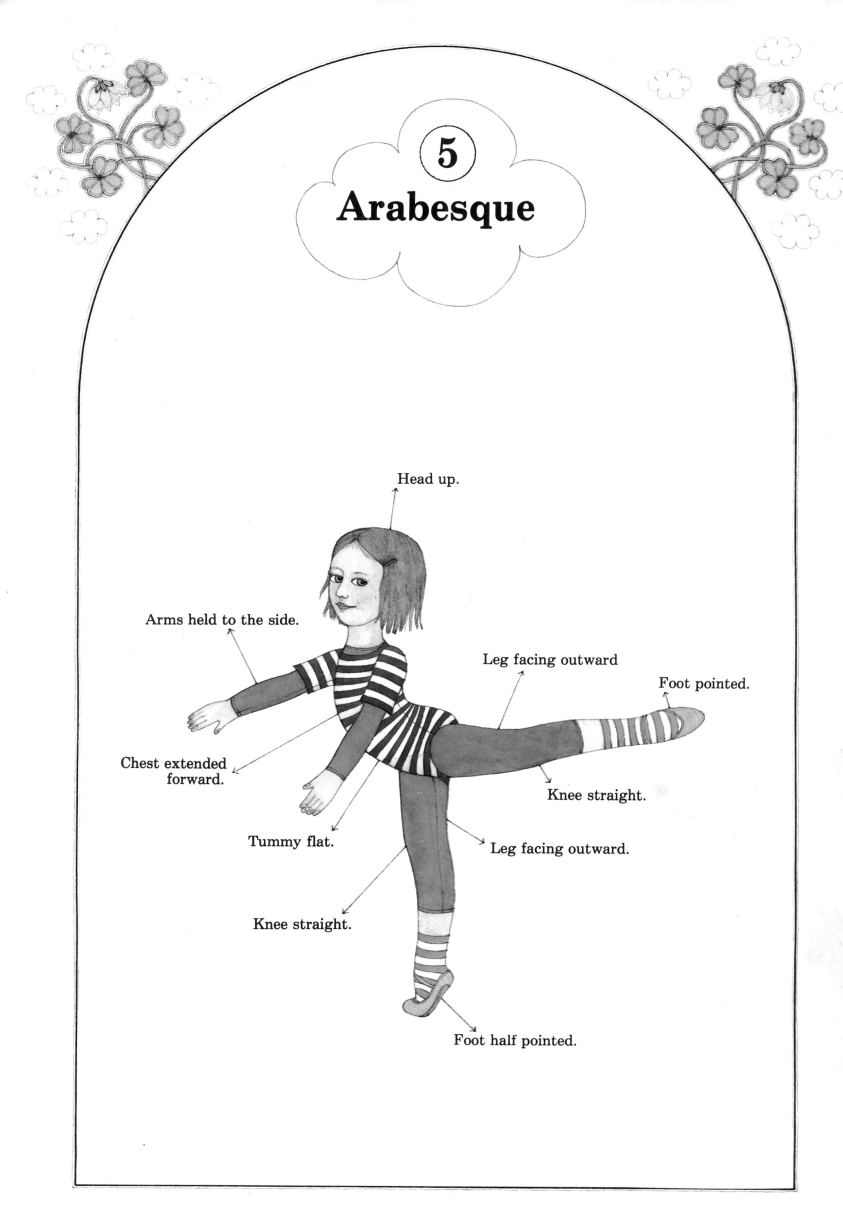

Head up.

Arms held to the side.

Leg facing outward

Foot pointed.

Chest extended
forward.

Knee straight.

Tummy flat.

Leg facing outward.

Knee straight.

Foot half pointed.

6

Little Jumps

Important!
Start every jump in a demi-plié.
Land after every jump in a demi-plié.
Always!

Or else from 2nd position.

From 1st position go into
a demi-plié and jump on the spot high
in the air. Straighten legs and point feet.
Land in a demi-plié lowering feet gently.
Press heels firmly to the ground.
Land as quietly as possible.

Knees straight.

Toes pointed.

Demi-plié.

1st position.

7
Changement

From 3rd position,
right foot in front, demi-plié, jump
high on the spot. Change feet in
mid-air and with the left foot in
front, gently land in 3rd position

9
Assemblé

A little jump from one leg on to two legs. 3rd position, left foot in front, demi-plié, slide right leg out to the side, jump high, and gently land in a demi-plié with both legs in 3rd position, right foot in front

(10)

Grand jeté

Run 2 steps—right-left—slide right leg through 1st position forward and extend upwards. Jump high and wide as if you were jumping over a large puddle. Land on the right leg in a demi-plié, body facing forward, left leg still extended to the back.

Draw the left leg up through 1st position, make 2 steps — left-right — draw the left leg through jump and land on the left leg.

Head up.

Ballet is fun!

2nd position.

Tummy pulled in.

Leg straight.

Toes pointed.

Leg straight.

Toes pointed.

Phew!

11
Splits

When all your muscles are fully trained and well warmed up, you can practise the splits. 3rd position, left foot in front, demi-plié, slide right leg out to the back, place hands on the floor. Stretch left leg out in front, bounce, and if possible do the splits and put arms in the 2nd position. To stand up, draw in the left leg, bring the right leg to the front, place right foot over the knee and stand up. The left leg closes in the back in 3rd position. Then practise the same on the other side.

By the way . . .

This is what a dancer looks like today

Here you can stick
a ballet photo
of yourself.

Little Ballet Dictionary
French-English

à coté . . . . . . a koteh . . . . . . sideways
adage . . . . . . adarge . . . . . . slowly
allegro . . . . . . allehgro . . . . . . fast
arabesque . . . . . . arabesk . . . . . . arabesque, ornament
assemblé . . . . . . assamblay . . . . . . join together
attitude . . . . . . attitood . . . . . . a standing position
balancé . . . . . . balãnssay . . . . . . balanced
battement . . . . . . batmãn . . . . . . a beating movement
bras . . . . . . bra . . . . . . arm
chainés . . . . . . shenay . . . . . . series of small turning steps
changement . . . . . . shanshmãn . . . . . . change
cou-de-pied . . . . . . koo deh peeay . . . . . . ankle joint
coupé . . . . . . kupeh . . . . . . cut
croisé . . . . . . krwahsay . . . . . . crossed over
degagé . . . . . . daygazhay . . . . . . free or unconstrained
demi . . . . . . demee . . . . . half
derrière . . . . . . dehreeair . . . . . . behind
dessous . . . . . . dessoo . . . . . . under
dessus . . . . . . dessu . . . . . . over
devant . . . . . . dehvãn . . . . . . in front
developpé . . . . . . devellopay . . . . . an unfolding of the leg
échappé . . . . . . ey-shah-pay . . . . . . escape, break away
effacé . . . . . . ehfahsay . . . . . turned to the side
en avant . . . . . . ãn ãvan . . . . . . forward
en dedans . . . . . . ãn dehdãn . . . . . . to the inside
en dehors . . . . . . ãn deh-or . . . . . . to the outside
en face . . . . . . ãn fahss . . . . . . facing
en suite . . . . . . ãn sweet . . . . . . in sequence
exercice . . . . . . aychs-air-sees . . . . . . exercise
fermer . . . . . . fair-may . . . . . . close
frappé . . . . . . frah-pay . . . . . . struck
glissade . . . . . . glee-sahd . . . . . . a slow, gliding step.
grand . . . . . . grãn . . . . . . large
grand jeté . . . . . . grãn zhetay . . . . . . large jump

For the pronunciation:
s . . . pretty hard
zh, sh very soft
ss . . . very hard
ãn . . . spoken
through the nose.

jambe . . . . . zhahmb . . . . . . leg
jeté . . . . . zhetay . . . . . . thrown, flung
ouvert . . . . . . ouvehr . . . . . . open
pas de basque . . . . . . pa de bahsk . . . . . . Basque step
pas de bourrée . . . . . . pa de booray . . . . . . Bourrée step
pas de chat . . . . . pa de sha . . . . . . cat like step
passé . . . . . . passay . . . . . pulled up
petit . . . . . . peh-tee . . . . . little
pied . . . . . pee-ay . . . . . foot
pirouette . . . . . . peer-oo-eht . . . . . . a turn on the toe
plié . . . . . plee-ay . . . . . bent
pointe . . . . . . pwănt . . . . . point
port de bras . . . . . . por dehbra . . . . . . carriage of the arms
position . . . . . . po-see-syon . . . . . . position
preparation . . . . . . pray-par-ahsyon . . . . . . preparation
relever . . . . . . reh-leh-vay . . . . . to rise up on the toes
révérence . . . . . ray-vair-ăns . . . . . . bow
rond . . . . . . rõn . . . . . round, circle
rond de jambe . . . . . . rõn deh zhamb . . . . . circling the leg
simple . . . . . sahmpl . . . . . simple
sissonne . . . . . . see-sonn . . . . a jump from both legs on to one leg.
tendu . . . . . tawndu . . . . . taut, stretched
tête . . . . . teht . . . . . head
tomber . . . . . . tombay . . . . . fall
tour . . . . . . toor . . . . . turn
à la barre . . . . . ah la bar . . . . . . at the barre
au milieu . . . . . . oh meel-yuh . . . . . . in the centre of the room

1	un	õn	one
2	deux	duh	two
3	trois	twa	three
4	quatre	kahtr	four
5	cinq	sank	five
6	six	seess	six
7	sept	set	seven
8	huit	weet	eight
9	neuf	nerf	nine
10	dix	deess	ten

By the way . . .
In French a pig
is called cochon . . . koshõn.
A cochonet . . . koshõnay . . .
is a piglet.

About Us

Heidi Sievert

chose the exercises for this book. Her father was a famous dancer. Her mother, Ossy Helken, has a ballet school in Frankfurt, West Germany. Heidi has danced ever since she could walk; by the time she was sixteen years old she was already in the Royal Ballet School in London. At nineteen she was the youngest prima ballerina in Germany and today she has a ballet school in Muenster, West Germany.

Antje Vogel

has painted since she's been able to think. This is her fourth book, others include *The Big Book for Growing Gardeners* and *There was once a Penguin*. She also danced at one time — for about ten years! Today she only dances from her desk to the stove, from the stove to her son and from her son back to her desk and, for her, that's a lot of fun!